Jack

gains two pounds every month.

Ashley

is the most sentimental of all.

Paul

dreams only of setting sail.

Jason

loves artistic activities.

LEARN-A-WORD BOOKS
IN ENGLISH, FRENCH & SPANISH

Animal Fun

227 Words in English,
French & Spanish

Text by Alain Grée
Illustrations by Luis Camps

DERRYDALE BOOKS • NEW YORK

Art copyright © 1979 by Casterman. English Translation copyright © 1986 by OBC, Inc. Originally published in French under the title *Les Farfeluches Aiment les Animaux*. All rights reserved. This 1986 edition is published by Derrydale Books, distributed by Crown Publishers, Inc., by arrangement with Casterman. Printed and Bound in Belgium.
Library of Congress Cataloging-in-Publication Data
Grée, Alain. Animal fun. (Learn-a-word books in English, French & Spanish). Translation of: Les farfeluches aiment les animaux. English, French, and Spanish.
　Summary: A group of kids known as "The Rascals" enjoy learning about animals. Includes brief running text and detailed illustrations with each item labeled in English, French, and Spanish. Also features games and related activities.
　　1. Animals—Juvenile literature.　2. Animals—Dictionaries—Polyglot.　3. Animals—Dictionaries, Juvenile.　4. Dictionaries, Polyglot.　[1. Animals.　2. Picture dictionaries, Polyglot]　I. Camps, Luis.　II. Title.　III. Series: Grée, Alain. Learn-a-word books in English, French & Spanish.
QL49.G72712　1986　　　591　　　86-8923　　　　　　ISBN 0-517-61497-9　　　hgfedcba

Like Cats and Dogs

When you like animals, it sure is fun to go and see the dogs and cats at the neighborhood pet shop. Hey, a newcomer has slipped in among the residents. Who could it be?

tiger kitten
chaton tigré
gatito tigre

Siamese
siamois
siamés

comb
peigne
peine

brush
brosse
cepillo

PET SHOP
CHENIL
PERRERA

pet food
pâtée
alimento

muzzle
muselière
bozal

German shepherd
berger allemand
pastor alemán

Afghan
lévrier afghan
afgano

collie
colley
perro pastor escocés

leash
laisse
correa

basset hound
basset
perro basset

fox terrier
fox
fóx terrier

4

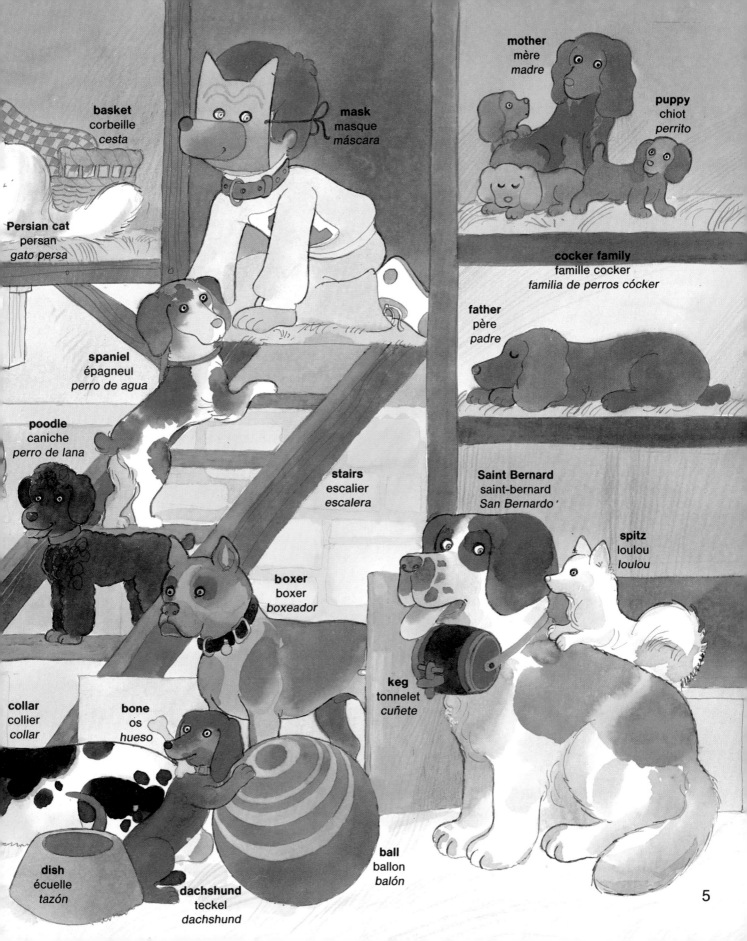

basket
corbeille
cesta

mask
masque
máscara

mother
mère
madre

puppy
chiot
perrito

Persian cat
persan
gato persa

cocker family
famille cocker
familia de perros cócker

father
père
padre

spaniel
épagneul
perro de agua

poodle
caniche
perro de lana

stairs
escalier
escalera

Saint Bernard
saint-bernard
San Bernardo '

spitz
loulou
loulou

boxer
boxer
boxeador

collar
collier
collar

bone
os
hueso

keg
tonnelet
cuñete

dish
écuelle
tazón

dachshund
teckel
dachshund

ball
ballon
balón

5

donkey
âne
asno

bull
taureau
toro

sheep
mouton
cordero

sow
truie
cerda

ewe
brebis
oveja

ram
bélier
carnero

rabbit
lapin
conejo

dog
chien
perro

donkey foal
ânon
asnico

cow
vache
vaca

mule
mulet
mula

From Donkey to Billy Goat

Our friends the Rascals have made up a matching game with the farm animals. But haven't they made sort of a mistake in cutting the cards?

horse
cheval
caballo

steer
boeuf
cabestro

mare
jument
yegua

pony
poulain
jaca

goat
chèvre
cabra

calf
veau
ternera

kid
chevreau
chivato

billy goat
bouc
chivo

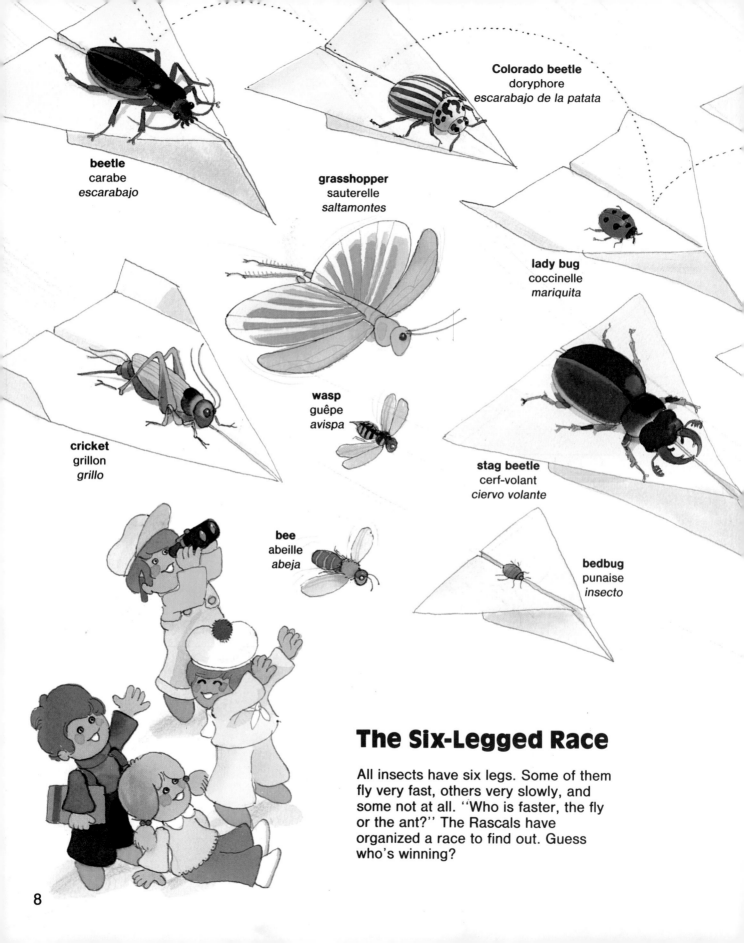

beetle
carabe
escarabajo

Colorado beetle
doryphore
escarabajo de la patata

grasshopper
sauterelle
saltamontes

lady bug
coccinelle
mariquita

cricket
grillon
grillo

wasp
guêpe
avispa

stag beetle
cerf-volant
ciervo volante

bee
abeille
abeja

bedbug
punaise
insecto

The Six-Legged Race

All insects have six legs. Some of them fly very fast, others very slowly, and some not at all. "Who is faster, the fly or the ant?" The Rascals have organized a race to find out. Guess who's winning?

8

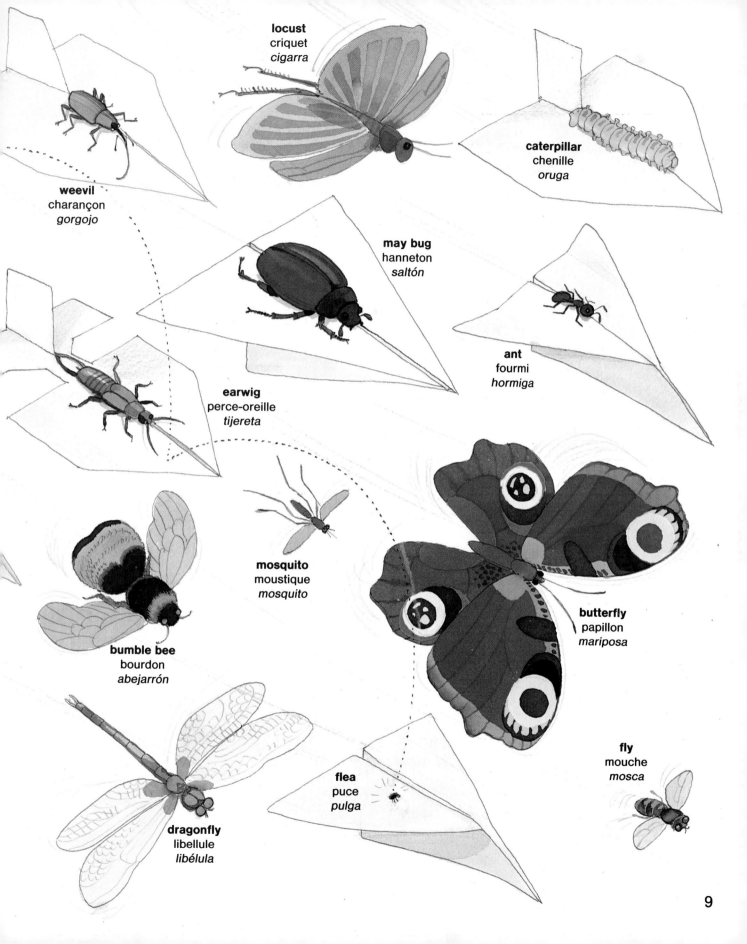

locust
criquet
cigarra

caterpillar
chenille
oruga

weevil
charançon
gorgojo

may bug
hanneton
saltón

ant
fourmi
hormiga

earwig
perce-oreille
tijereta

mosquito
moustique
mosquito

butterfly
papillon
mariposa

bumble bee
bourdon
abejarrón

dragonfly
libellule
libélula

flea
puce
pulga

fly
mouche
mosca

9

wheel
roue
rueda

cap
casquette
gorro

otter
loutre
nutria

wood file
rape
raspador

spider
araignée
araña

jerboa
gerboise
jerbo

ermine
hermine
armiño

pump
pompe
bomba

inner tube
chambre à air
cámara

viper
vipère
víbora

shrew-mouse
musaraigne
musaraña

patches
pièces
remiendas

snails
escargots
caracoles

frog
grenouille
rana

tortoise
tortue
tortuga

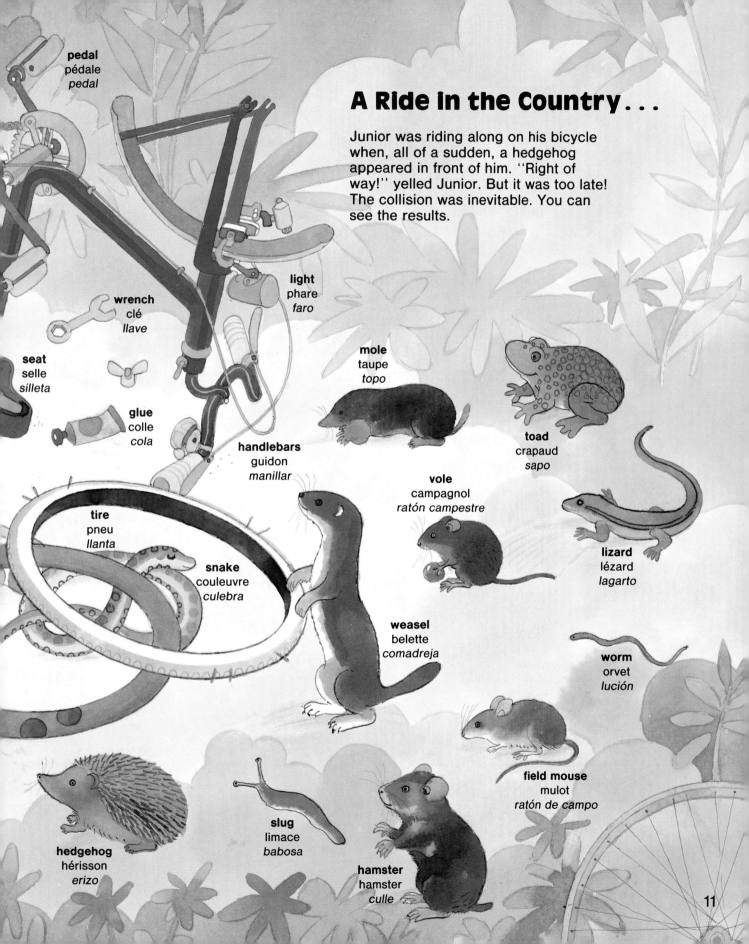

pedal
pédale
pedal

A Ride in the Country...

Junior was riding along on his bicycle when, all of a sudden, a hedgehog appeared in front of him. "Right of way!" yelled Junior. But it was too late! The collision was inevitable. You can see the results.

wrench
clé
llave

light
phare
faro

seat
selle
silleta

mole
taupe
topo

toad
crapaud
sapo

glue
colle
cola

handlebars
guidon
manillar

vole
campagnol
ratón campestre

lizard
lézard
lagarto

tire
pneu
llanta

snake
couleuvre
culebra

weasel
belette
comadreja

worm
orvet
lución

field mouse
mulot
ratón de campo

hedgehog
hérisson
erizo

slug
limace
babosa

hamster
hamster
culle

11

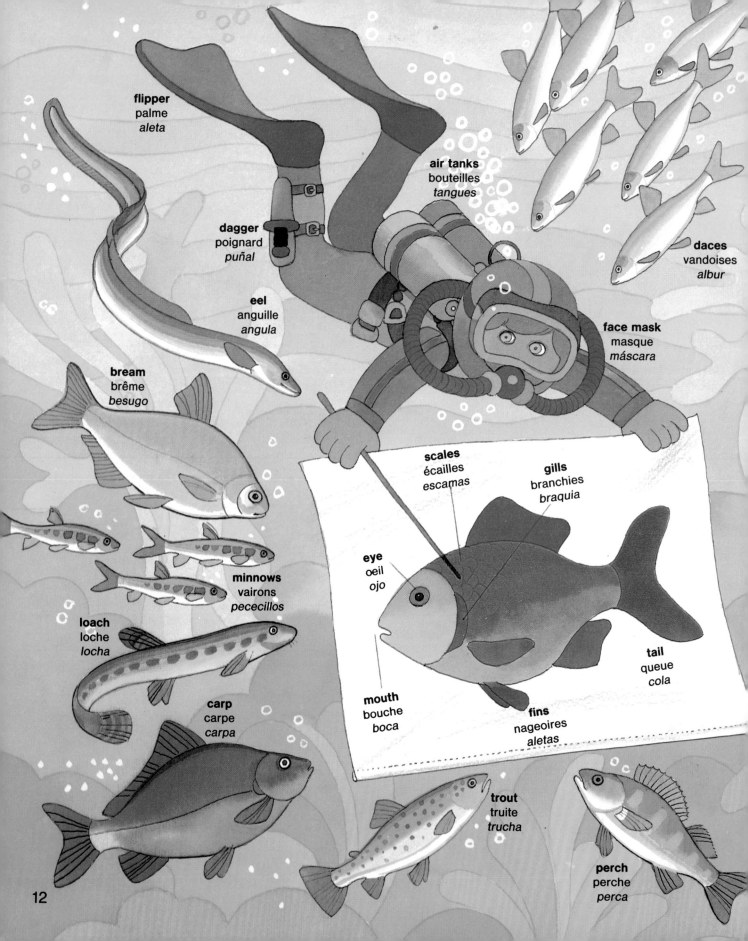

flipper
palme
aleta

air tanks
bouteilles
tangues

daces
vandoises
albur

dagger
poignard
puñal

eel
anguille
angula

face mask
masque
máscara

bream
brême
besugo

scales
écailles
escamas

gills
branchies
braquia

eye
oeil
ojo

minnows
vairons
pececillos

loach
loche
locha

tail
queue
cola

mouth
bouche
boca

carp
carpe
carpa

fins
nageoires
aletas

trout
truite
trucha

perch
perche
perca

12

roaches
gardons
escarchos

snorkle
tuba
tubillo de buceo

catfish
barbeaux
barbo

chubs
chabots
cotos

camera
caméra
cámara

belt
ceinture
cinturón

salmon
saumon
salmón

wet suit
combinaison
traje de buceo

tench
tanche
tenca

gudgeons
goujons
gobios

sturgeon
esturgeon
esturrión

bleaks
ablettes
brecas

pike
brochet
sollo

Say It with Bubbles

On Sunday, the Rascals decided to play school with the fish in the river. First lesson: the parts of the body. Where are the scales? If you know the answer, raise your fin!

Our Feathered Friends

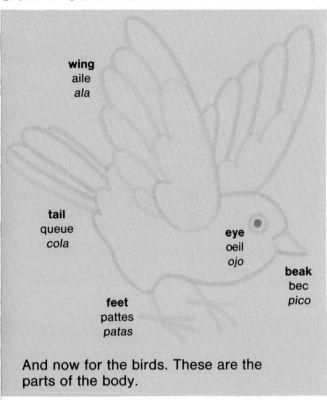

wing
aile
ala

tail
queue
cola

eye
oeil
ojo

beak
bec
pico

feet
pattes
patas

And now for the birds. These are the parts of the body.

woodpecker
pivert
picaposte

raven
corbeau
cuervo

kingfisher
martin-pêcheur
martín-pescador

gull
mouette
gaviota

Hey, someone lost a feather. And here's another!

magpie
pie
urraca

owl
chouette
buho

pigeon
pigeon
paloma

Mrs. Magpie shakes her head: "It's not mine. Look next door."

partridge
perdrix
perdiz

parrot
perroquet
loro

sparrow
moineau
gorrión

Not here either. No one has lost anything. Unless of course . . . it's . . .

14

eagle
aigle
águila

parakeet
perruche
periquito

robin
rouge gorge
petirrojo

Here's yet another one. Someone's sure leaving his things all over the place this morning.

swallow
hirondelle
golondrina

nightingale
rossignol
ruiseñor

blackbird
merle
merla

Whose is this green feather? No one answers. Is it yours, nightingale?

spear
lance
lanza

necklace
collier
collar

peace pipe
calumet
pipa de la paz

feathers
plumes
plumas

bow
arc
arco

mocassin
mocassin
mocasín

hatchet
hache
hacha

arrows
flèches
flechas

. . . a joke by the Rascal tribe!

A Special Report

The Rascals are making a special report for the school paper from the barnyard. "Ladies and gentlemen, would you mind saying a few words for our listeners?"

Rescue in the Forest

"Fire, fire! The forest is burning." The frightened animals run in every direction to get away from the flames. Luckily the Rascals have quickly built a raft. Everyone will be rescued just in time!

roe deer
chevreuil
corza

weasel
putois
mofeta

crate
caisse
caja

squirrel
ecureuil
ardilla

pole
perche
palo

doe
biche
cierva

fox
renard
zorro

deer
daim
gamo

net
épuisette
red

skunk
blaireau
zorillo

wolf
loup
lobo

18

smoke
fumée
humo

roebuck
cerf
ciervo

wild boar
sanglier
jabalí

dormouse
loir
lirón

hare
lièvre
liebre

plank
planche
tabla

racoon
raton-laveur
mapache

beaver
castor
castor

sable
martre
cebellina

marten
fouine
macta

mouse
souris
ratón

barrel
tonneau
barril

19

The Match-Up Game

The purpose of this game is to match up pairs (male and female) of animals. It is played by a group, with one die. The order of players is chosen at random, and the first player throws the die to designate the column (from 1 to 6). He or she then throws the die a second time and counts the circles, starting from the top.

NOTE: If the number on the second roll is over 4, continue counting from bottom to top.

EXAMPLE: first throw = 3 (3rd. column); second throw = 5, count: wild sow, boar, ewe, drake, and back up to ewe. Then the player has to find the animal that is the mate of the ewe. In our example the answer would be "ram." If the player answers right the first time, he or she gets a point. Then it's the next player's turn.

ALSO: Earning 6 points allows the player to go again. The first player to reach 10 points wins.

(The answers are in the back of the book.)

20

1

horse
cheval
caballo

wild boar
sanglier
jabalí

goat
chèvre
chivo

cow
vache
vaca

2

gander
jars
ganso

bull
taureau
toro

rooster
coq
gallo

she wolf
louve
loba

3

wild sow
laie
jabalina

boar
verrat
cochino

ewe
brebis
oveja

drake
canard
pato

4

billy goat
bouc
chivo

doe hare
hase
liebrina

stag
cerf
ciervo

hen
poule
gallina

5

wolf
loup
lobo

goose
oie
ganso

mare
jument
yegua

doe
biche
cierva

6

ram
bélier
carnero

hare
lièvre
liebre

duck
cane
pata

sow
truie
cochina

21

Justine

is already a perfect homemaker.

Patrick

fights imaginary bandits.

Rudy

is only happy with a hammer in his hand.

Junior

is seventy-five pounds of muscle.

Max

hopes to be a pilot someday.

Peter

is more absent-minded than clumsy.